Museum Guide for Temporary Washingtonians

Museum Guide for Temporary Washingtonians

Hoon-Jeong Hwang

ISBN: 978-1-62429-244-6

Printed through Opus Self-Publishing Services
Located at:
Politics and Prose Bookstore
5015 Connecticut Ave. NW
Washington, D.C. 20008
www.politics-prose.com / / (202) 364-1919

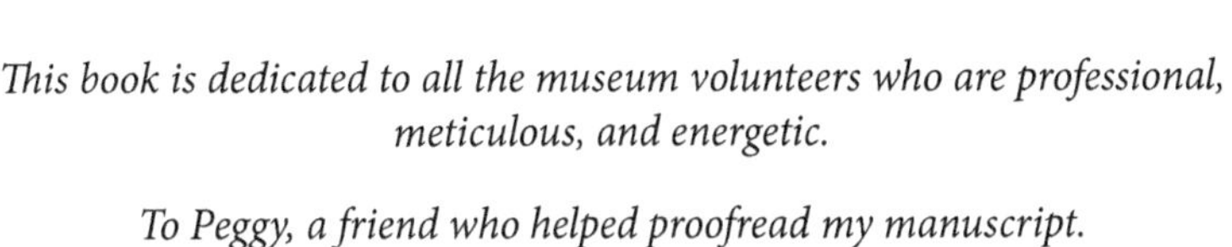

This book is dedicated to all the museum volunteers who are professional, meticulous, and energetic.

To Peggy, a friend who helped proofread my manuscript.

And lastly, to my parents, Bryan, Andy, and my husband, Jin, for their incredible support and love.

Table of Contents

Museum Guide for Temporary Washingtonians

Hoon-Jeong Hwang

Introduction

One of the things that I love about living in the Washington D.C. area is the variety of activities the city has to offer. You can wander around the National Mall, enjoy the cherry blossoms nestled in tight clusters in spring, tour the U.S. Capitol Building and its towering dome, and even score a visit to the Senate and House galleries when Congress is in session. But best of all, you have access to some of the greatest museums in the world. This guidebook introduces forty-one of the best museums in D.C.

I am relatively new to D.C and still view the city with fresh eyes. Everything here is marvelous, even the dog poop. The people are nice and the streets are clean. But I've also noticed that Washingtonians are a hectic and busy people—so much so that it has been difficult for me to make true friends. So, whenever I feel lonesome, I go to museums. They talk to me like an intimate friend and comfort me. As with the stories they share with me, I felt the need to tell others about my wonderful experiences. It is aimed at temporary Washingtonians—from the weekend tourist to the newcomers on an extended stay—who crave the unique, the curious, the distinctive, all the things a modern city has to offer. I don't want to be a cultural snob, or discuss trends, or reiterate information that is available online. I hope that what I've seen and felt for the last four years in this beautiful city merits sharing with others who are in search of the treasures of Washington.

Unlike New York, Boston, and Philadelphia, Washington D.C is a planned city. The District of Columbia was founded in 1771 as the permanent seat of government of the new United States of America. The states of Maryland and Virginia donated land to form the federal district, which initially covered the existing colonial settlements of Georgetown and Alexandria. Thus, the first shape of city was a diamond. However, in 1846, Congress returned the land ceded by Virginia and the diamond shape was truncated.

In 1791, President Washington commissioned Pierre Charles L'Enfant, a French-born architect and city planner, to design the new capital. The L'Enfant Plan featured broad streets and avenues radiating out from rectangles, providing room for open space and landscaping. He based his design on the plans of cities such as Paris, Amsterdam, Karlsruhe, and Milan. Surprisingly, President Washington dismissed L'Enfant in March 1792 due to conflicts with the three commissioners appointed to supervise the capital's construction. Andrew Ellicott, who had worked with L'Enfant surveying the city, was then tasked with completing the design. Though Ellicott made revisions to the original plans – including changes to some street patterns – L'Enfant is still credited with the overall design of the city. (From Wikipedia)

The Smithsonian Museums

Where to start:

The Smithsonian Institution building, also known as The Castle, because it looks like a medieval castle from the outside.

1000 Jefferson Drive SW
8:30 a.m. - 5:30 p.m.
Metro: Smithsonian (Mall exit)

Note: L'Enfant Plaza, Smithsonian, Archives, Federal Triangle, and Metro Center are the main Metro stations for most museum visits.

The Castle not only acts as the grand centerpiece for the Smithsonian Institution but is also the Visitor Center and administrative offices for the vast group of Smithsonian museums on the National Mall. The Castle offers an exhibition on its own history that is worth seeing. It also has a wonderful garden filled with seasonal blooming flowers. Hundreds of purple magnolias greet visitors every spring.

If you want insider tips on how to enjoy your time on the Mall, the best way is to ask volunteers. They will answer your questions with terrific enthusiasm. (The Smithsonian museum group has a great number of volunteers who are professional as well as enthusiastic to help others.)

Who was James Smithson?

James Smithson was a founding donor of the Smithsonian museums. An English chemist and mineralogist, he pursued a range of interests in the sciences, including applied mechanics. Toward the end of his life, he left his fortune to the United States, which he had never visited, for the founding of an institution committed to "the increase and diffusion of knowledge among men." Smithson died in Genoa, Italy in 1829, although his remains were brought to the United States in 1904.

NATIONAL MUSEUM of the AMERICAN INDIAN
American Indian
Smithsonian
NATIONAL MUSEUM of the AMERICAN INDIAN
Smithsonian
Smithsonian

Smithsonian National Museum of the American Indian

4th St & Independence Avenue SW
10:00 a.m. – 5:30 p.m.
Metro: L'Enfant Station

Originally, the American continent belonged to its native population. At the National Museum of the American Indian, you can learn about the tribes, culture, and lives of these indigenous people who called the United States, Canada, Mexico, Central America, and South America home for many centuries before the arrival of Europeans. The landscape and architecture of the museum was designed to evoke a sense of the natural environment that existed prior to European contact.

Begin your visit in the Lelawi Theatre, located on the 4th level, which features a 13-minute film celebrating the vitality and diversity of Native life. I like the ceiling which changes to a screen as soon as the movie starts. Next stop on the tour is "Nation to Nation," an exhibition that explains the treaties between the United States and American Indian Nations. The exhibition makes clear that these treaties were broken by the United States. I also love to spend time on the exhibits of crafts and beadwork

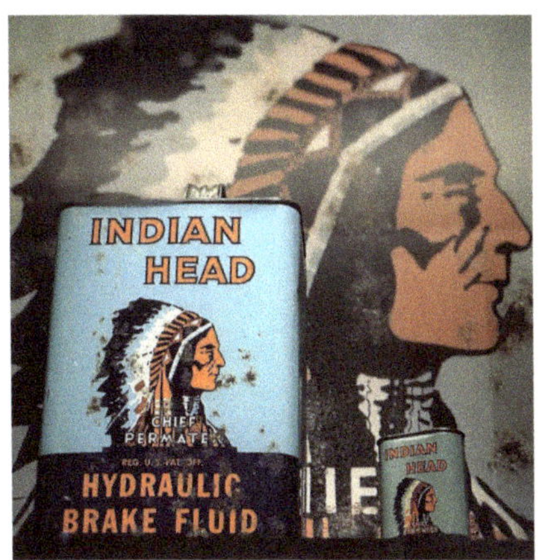

that highlight the artistry and ingenuity of American Indians. They beautifully illustrate the artists' interpretation of the world around them and their various relationships with the United States. One striking exhibit that I'll never forget is a pair of black-rimmed Mary Jane shoes which were made in collaboration with luxury shoe brand, Christian Louboutin. They are sky blue with colorful beads and adore them.

(Jamie Okuma, Transitions 1&2, 2012)

I was surprised to learn to what extent American Indian influence has had on US culture and commerce. I had not known that a great number of US commercial products synonymous with the nation and its values had their origins in American Indian traditions, stories, and tragic history. After a short tour, you realize how embedded American Indians are in the identity of the United States.

If you're hungry after the tour or in need of a snack, I recommend dropping by Mitsam, the museum cafe, which has scrumptious meals and snacks. It also has a huge space where various American Indian tribal flags are displayed.

The National Museum of the American Indian is a perfect place for not only American history fans but also families with little kids. I heartily recommend the museum's Imaginations Activity Center, which provides wonderful programs for children.

Smithsonian National Air and Space Museum

600 Independence Avenue SW
10:00 a.m. - 5:30 p.m.
Metro: L'Enfant Station

The National Air and Space Museum is such a popular destination for both adults and children that you have to line up for entry. Who are the visitors? Adults who once dreamed of being an astronaut, but also little kids whose futures might be shaped by their experiences at this thrilling museum. The museum's many rare treasures include the Apollo 11 command module from the first moon landing, rocks brought back from

the moon by the Apollo 17 astronauts, and the original Wright brothers' flier. Many of their exhibits are interactive, and sky shows at the Albert Einstein Planetarium and the five-story high IMAX movie theater only add to the experience. Special family activities are offered regularly, including the chance to look through the museum's giant telescope. Please keep in mind that this museum is in the middle of huge renovation right now and some galleries are temporarily closed.

Unlike some other Smithsonian museums, the Air and Space has a branch just outside of D.C. The Udvar-Hazy Center, near Dulles Airport,

is a hangar-style building with many aircrafts on display, including such famous planes as the Enola Gay, the Lockheed SR-71 Blackbird, and the Caudron G.4, used as a reconnaissance bomber during World War I and is only one of two that still exist. If you are an aircraft enthusiast, you will be mesmerized by the magnitude of the Udvar-Hazy Center and its numerous aircraft on exhibit. It's also home to the Discovery Space Shuttle! However, if you are pressed for time and must choose one, the Air and Space Museum on the National Mall is a must-see.

Yayoi Kusama *Pumpkin*, 2016

Jimmie Durham *Still Life with Spirit and Xitle*, 2007

Hirshhorn Museum and Sculpture Garden

Independence Avenue & 7th Street SW
10:00 a.m. - .5:30 p.m.
Metro: Smithsonian

The Hirshhorn Museum and Sculpture Garden is one of my favorite museums in D.C. I love it for its experimental approach to contemporary art. Paintings, videos, digital performances, and technological pieces are regularly on view. By the entrance is a sculpture of a car crushed under the weight of 9-ton boulder with a comical smiley face painted on it. *Titled Still Life with Spirit and Xitle*, it is one of the most well-known works of art by artist Jimmie Durham, a sculptor famous for his sense of humor and irreverence. *The Pumpkin,* a yellow and black sculpture in the shape of a pumpkin designed by the acclaimed Japanese artist Yayoi Kusama, also greets visitors on arrival. It was recently moved to the Sculpture Garden.

In 2017, many young Washingtonians visited Yayoi Kusama's exhibition at the Hirshhorn. The artist has produced more than 20 distinct "Infinity Mirror Rooms", and the Hirshhorn —the first museum to focus on this pioneering body of work—presented six of them, the most ever shown together. A description from the Hirschhorn's website summarizes the incredible exhibition: "Ranging from peep-show-like chambers to multimedia installations, each of Yayoi Kusama's kaleidoscopic environments provides the chance to step into an illusion of infinite space. The rooms also provided an opportunity to examine the artist's central themes, such as the celebration of life and its aftermath."

This phenomenal museum continuously introduces new artists to visitors. Japanese artist Hiroshi Sugimoto recently transformed the museum lobby with designs inspired by a medieval Japanese nutmeg tree and its mass of roots. The look and feel extended even further to the recently renovated furnishings, from the welcome desks to the gorgeous 20 foot metal coffee bar that serves up Dolcezza Coffee and Gelato. Visitors also won't want to miss a prismatic light sculpture by Icelandic artist Olafur Eliasson.

I have a habit of strolling in the sculpture garden early on Sunday mornings, where I make a wish in front of the Wish Tree, a public art installation by Yoko Ono, who was the wife of John Lennon, a singer in the Beatles. Every summer through Labor Day, visitors are invited to the sculpture garden to tie their written wishes to the branches of the tree. I never forget to write a wish for my family.

Yoko Ono *Wish Tree*, 2007

Yayoi Kusama *Infinity Mirror Room-Phalli's Field*, 1965/2016

SAAM
Portrait

Smithsonian American Art Museum and National Portrait Gallery

8th Avenue & F Street NW
11:00 a.m. - 7:00 p.m.
Metro: Gallery Place/ Chinatown Station

Located in vibrant downtown D.C., the Smithsonian American Art Museum shares this National Historic Landmark building with the National Portrait Gallery. Designed by the globally renowned architect Norman Foster, the enclosed courtyard provides a distinctive, contemporary accent to the museums' Greek revival appearance. These museums open earlier and close later than the other museums in D.C., which means that you can plan for your tour with more flexibility and less haste. The Smithsonian American Art Museum has can't-miss exhibits dealing with American history and artworks. The collections at the Portrait Gallery include historic figures, 20th century leaders, entertainers, and popular sports figures.

Without question, the current highlights at the Portrait Gallery are portraits of President Barack Obama and former First Lady Michelle Obama. Large crowds gather and take pictures daily of these newly unveiled portraits. Before they went on display, many tourists had not regarded this 50 year old museum as an important attraction in D.C. However, as with many other things, the Obamas changed people's views. They made the National Portrait of Gallery hot and hip. More than 2.3 million visitors came through to see the only these paintings.

Kehinde Wiley
President Barack Obama, 2018

When I first encountered President Obama surrounded by a mass of flowers, I felt that the portrait, painted by artist Kehinde Wiley, captured his vibrant life.

When I saw Michelle set against a simple blue background wearing a geometrically patterned mixed-color dress, her face rendered in shades of gray, I was totally hooked by a different kind of beauty. The artist's name is Amy Sherald. She and Wiley are both African American. Both painters represent a new generation of African American artists telling African American stories in contemporary ways, I am curious to see who is going to paint President Donald Trump's portrait for the Gallery.

Let's move on to the American Art Museum. Nineteenth century works that capture the original American landscape are favorites here, especially Thomas Moran's The Grand Canyon of the Yellowstone. A modernization of sorts is located just upstairs. I always take photos in front of Nam June Paik's video art installation, Electronic Superhighway. Nam June Paik was a Korean American who was the originator of video art. As a Korean, I am proud that he was a pioneer of a new

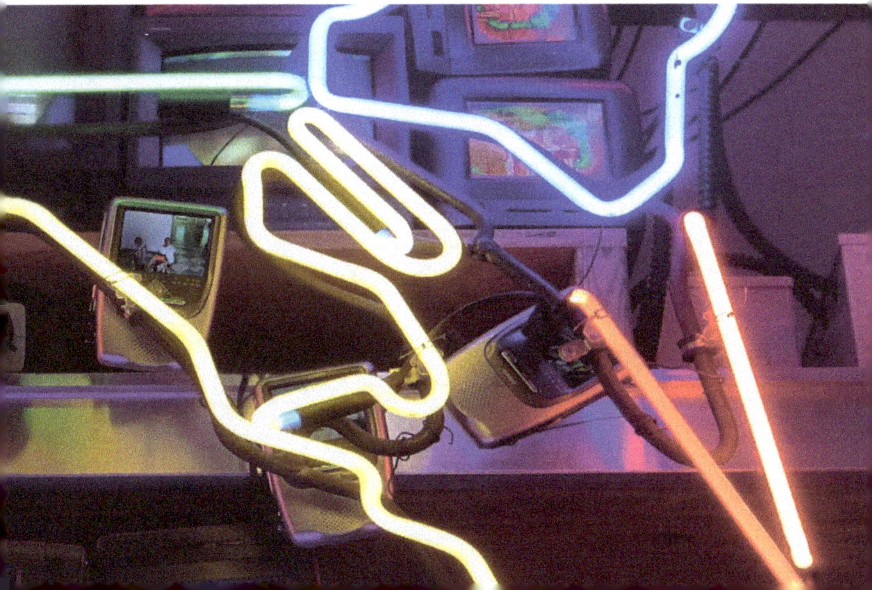

Nam June Paik *Electronic Superhighway: Continental U.S., Alaska, Hawaii*, 1995

era of visual art. Paik's artwork, fully-titled Electronic Superhighway: Continental U.S., Alaska, Hawaii, illustrates his interpretation of the United States through media technology, where he had immigrated at 16 years old. Paik is credited with the first use of the term "electronic superhighway" in the 1970s. Electronic Superhighway — constructed of 336 televisions, 50 DVD players, 3,750 feet of cable, and 575 feet of multicolored neon tubing —is a testament to Paik's prescience of the future. He already knew that advanced technology could change the world.

The video clips in Electronic Superhighway: Continental U.S., Alaska, Hawaii, remind us that individual states have distinctive identities and original cultures. The sheer size of the installation arouses a visceral reaction from visitors when they first see it. It replicates the shock the artist must have experienced when he encountered the American highway system. Interestingly, the concepts he chose to represent each state are based on his understanding through films and popular TV shows and personal connections. For example, The Wizard of Oz is used for Kansas, while well-known composer John Cage represents Paik's idea of Massachusetts. Do you know that a camera is still working to show visitors the right moment in the Smithsonian American Art Museum?

If you are interested in English conversation about American history and art, please come over to this museum at 10 a.m. on Fridays and sit in the lobby before opening time. You will meet wonderful museum workers who will guide you as you explore a profound new world.

Thanks to a generous donation from the Henry Luce Foundation, you can also enjoy more than 3000 art works in the Luce Foundation Center that would otherwise be housed in offsite storage. Come explore either on your own or with a docent the Center's sixty-four glass cases filled with paintings, sculptures, and many crafts including bronze, metals, and jewelry. The Luce Foundation Center also provides public programs and information about the collection. Lastly, the Explore Gallery, designed for children ages 1½ to 8 years, offers a host of daily activities, including stories about the subjects of the paintings at 11:45 a.m., Tuesdays to Sundays.

Renwick Gallery

Pennsylvania Avenue & 17th Street NW
10:00 a.m. - 5:30 p.m.
Metro: Farragut West

An Extension of the American Art Museum, the Renwick Gallery focuses on contemporary crafts and decorative art. It is housed in a National Historic Landmark building that was begun in 1859 on Pennsylvania Avenue, originally housing the Corcoran Gallery of Art.

Many of the pieces are distinctly unique. This museum prefers to display special exhibitions rather than a permanent collection. Last year, "No Spectators, The Art of Burning Man" was a very popular exhibit. It brought for the first time the large-scale work from Nevada's annual Burning Man Festival to the nation's capital. The immersive, room-sized installations were powerful and touching.

The most fascinating artwork is the temple made with pieces of wood on which people have written stories about their deceased loved ones. I cried and cried when I first came across it and felt very fortunate to have my family members standing by my side. This exhibit is still on display.

Left: David Best *Temple for No Spectators,* 2018
Right: Marco Cochrane *Truth is Beauty,* 2017

Who was James Renwick Jr.?

James Renwick Jr. was an American architect who lived during the 19th century. Renwick was not formally trained as an architect, but his ability and interest in designing buildings were nurtured through a cultural education that included architectural history. In 1846, Renwick won a competition for the design of the Smithsonian Institution Building. The Castle was designed in the Romanesque style, which influenced the Gothic revival style in the United States.

Freer Gallery of Art and Arthur M. Sackler Gallery

1050 Independence Avenue NW
10:00 a.m. - 5:30 p.m.
Metro: Smithsonian

The Freer and the Arthur M. Sackler galleries are located next door to each other. Together they house some of the best artifacts of Asian art in the world. The Freer Gallery of Art opened to the public in 1923 as the first art museum on the National Mall. Nearly a century later, they continue to explore the connections among founding gifts of Asian and American art there. The Arthur M. Sackler Gallery opened as an essential counterpoint to the Freer Gallery in 1987. "Two museums, one destination" is their slogan.

At the turn of the 20th century, European art dominated the market. However, Charles Lang Freer, a wealthy self-made businessman and collector was instrumental in opening a new horizon for Asian art. An eclectic cross-cultural collection showcased in a Renaissance-style palace is the result of this mission. More than 100 years after Freer amassed his collection, his namesake art gallery has retained its eclectic character. In the blue and gold Peacock Room, the shelves are filled with ceramics from throughout Asia. I love the Freer Gallery because it perfectly embodies Freer's passion for art. The Freer Gallery is also unique in that it links the art of American painter James McNeill Whistler to Asian art.

Amazed by Whistler's paintings and artistic philosophy, Freer eventually became one of his patrons. Whistler's drew inspiration for his paintings from Japanese wood -block prints, which in turn ignited Freer's interest in collecting Asian art. The Whistler connection adds another extraordinary note to this museum.

James McNeill Whistler *Harmony in Blue and Gold: The Peacock Room*, 1877

Contrary to the Freer Gallery (galleries 1-19) where each room is named for the geographic origin of the art within (China, Korea and so on), the Sackler Gallery (galleries 20-30) provides special exhibitions based on a particular subject. Asia is a grand continent filled with multiple religions, various ethnic backgrounds, and thousands of years of history, therefore it is hard to reduce to a one-word defintion what the art of Asia is like.

At the Sackler, you'll find elegant portraits of Chinese empresses in the Forbidden City, the fabled aromatics from Yemen, Buddhas from across Asia, and animal-shaped vessels from ancient Iran all at the same time.

Tibetan Buddhist Shrine Room from the Alice S. Kandell Collection

National Museum of African Art

950 Independence Avenue SW
10:00 a.m. - 5:30 p.m.
Metro: Smithsonian

This museum really sweeps me off my feet. The strength of collection lies in its immeasurable depth and diversity from ancient to contemporary African art. Donated to the museum in 2005, the Walt Disney-Tishman Collection is known for unique and rare works of traditional African art from throughout sub-Saharan Africa. The collection has been instrumental in defining the field of African art history in the United States and abroad. In 1963, during the height of the civil rights movement, retired U.S Foreign Service officer Warren M. Robbins established a center for cross-cultural understanding to show the rich creative heritage of Africa. The following year, he expanded his vision and opened the Museum of African Art. By an act of Congress, this small beginning blossomed to become home to more than 12,000 works of art. Enjoy the journey through time!

One artwork you must see is the Rainbow Serpent constructed from recycled jerry cans, which are used for storing gasoline. This work addresses the horror of the transatlantic slave trade which happened centuries ago and its economic equivalents today. The circular image of the rainbow serpent swallowing its tail is a powerful symbol among Fon and Yoruba peoples in Benin and Nigeria, where it refers to spiritual forces and positive ideas about fertility, prosperity, and the eternal cycle of life.

Romuald Hazoumè *Rainbow Serpent*, 2007

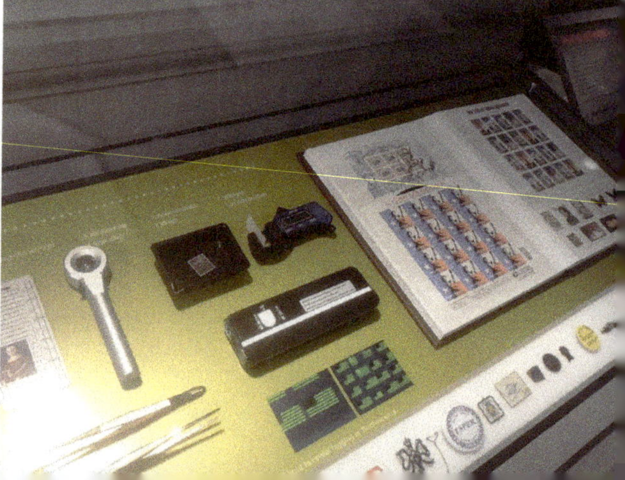

National Postal Museum

2 Massachusetts Avenue NE
10:00 a.m. - 5:30 p.m.
Metro: Union Station

If I have to choose my favorite specialized museum in D.C., it would be the National Postal Museum, without hesitation. The National Postal Museum stores the National Philatelic Collection and features wonderful rare historic artifacts from U.S. Postal history, including stamps and assorted vehicles used for delivering mail. It hosts interactive displays, and exhibits, including a delightful one on the Pony Express.

Named after its primary benefactor, the William H. Gross Stamp Gallery is the world's largest gallery dedicated to philately. As visitors move through six thematic areas, stunning interactive displays reveal amazing stories that unfold from the museum's unparalleled collection.

The museum boasts such splendid sights as the Havilland DH-4 and the Stinson Reliant, historic airplanes that flew mail across the country, as well as the Concord Mail Coach, Mud Wagon, Screen Wagon, and Central America Steamer, which carried mail on long destinations via railroad and horse-drawn carriage. At a place for the young and the young at heart, visitors can design their own stamps, write and mail a postcard, sit in the cab of a postal truck, ride in a stagecoach, or sort packages like folks in the mail room.

Smithsonian National Museum of African American History and Culture

1400 Constitution Avenue NW
10:00 a.m. - 5:30 p.m.
Free, with ticket required at certain times (http://www.nmaahc.si.edu)
Metro: Federal Triangle

Spend a full day at this fascinating museum enjoying historic and cultural artifacts from the early 15th century through to the present. For the best experience, begin your visit on C3, the lowest level. When you step off the elevator, you are immediately immersed in a visually arresting and powerful exhibit that explores the story of the transatlantic slave trade, a commercial and economic enterprise in which Africans were forcibly seized from their homes and shipped to Europe and the Americas to labor as slaves. You will see the small iron shackles which were used to restrain children; you will see the names, countries and cargo of every slave ship that participated in the transatlantic slave trade on the walls; and you will come across a haunting video of West Africa coast, which used to be called the Slave Coast. There are also exhibits about the vicious southern slave trade and about Harriet Tubman, an escaped slave who helped to lead many African Americans to freedom on the Underground Railroad. As you make your way through the 20th century, you will encounter a solemn room where lies the original coffin of 14 -year- old Emmett Till, tortured and killed in 1955 for allegedly whistling at a white woman. There is also a stool from the Woolworth

lunch counter in Greensboro where young African Americans staged a four month sit-in to protest segregation in 1960. When you walk further, you will see an exhibit about changing America which covers recent American history from the death of Martin Luther King Jr. through to the second presidential term of Barack Obama.

The top floor of the museum hosts a stunning and interactive array of exhibits that celebrate and highlight the enormous contributions African Americans have made to the visual arts, pop music, and other forms of cultural expression. The trumpet owned by Louis Armstrong and Chuck Berry's 1973 red Cadillac are a few of the thrilling cultural artifacts on display.

Take the escalator down one floor to the Community Galleries, where the theme is "Making a Way Out of No Way." The galleries present a history of African American military service from the American Revolution through to the Iraq War. Another highlight is "Sports." Look for the shirt that Tiger Woods was wearing the first time he won the Masters Golf Tournament and Muhammad Ali's boxing gloves and robe. There are exhibits honoring Michael Jordan and the statue of Olympians Tommie Smith and Juan Carlos who respectively won gold and bronze medals at the 1968 Olympics.

Designed by David Adjaye and Philip Freelon, the National Museum of African American History and Culture is a work of art. The design of the building is inspired by the three-tiered crowns found in African Yoruba sculpture. The exterior is wrapped in an ornamental bronze metal latticework. With this effect, Adjaye pays homage to the intricate ironwork crafted by enslaved African Americans.

Smithsonian National Museum of American History

1300 Constitution Avenue NW (between 12th and 14th Street)
10:00 a.m. - 5:30 p.m.
Metro: Smithsonian

The Museum of American History is the best D.C. museum when it comes to bringing your history books to life. You will learn about many of the important events that helped shape the United States of America. The museum hosts an amazing exhibit of dresses worn by the First Ladies and has on display the original Star-Spangled Banner. Since I am always overwhelmed by the museum's sheer size, I have compiled a list of must-see sights to assist visitors in navigating its impressive collections.

Must-See Sights

1. **Star-Spangled Banner, 1814 (2 Center)** The flag that flew over Fort McHenry near Baltimore and inspired Francis Scott Key to pen the lyrics that became the national anthem.
2. **Greensboro Lunch Counter, 1960 (2 East)** In 1960, four African American students protested Jim Crow laws at this original section of the F.W. Woolworth lunch counter in Greensboro, North Carolina.
3. **Ruby Slippers, 1939 (3 West)** The ruby slippers are the magic pair of shoes worn by Dorothy Gale as played by Judy Garland in the 1939 MGM musical movie "The Wizard of Oz." These iconic slippers have a new home in a large gallery meant to evoke Emerald City. Additional artifacts from the film are on display.
4. **Thomas Jefferson's Desk, 1776 (3 center) The American Presidency.**
5. **Michelle Obama's inaugural Gown, 2013 (3 Center) First Ladies at the Smithsonian.**
6. **George Washington's Uniform, 1789 (3 East) The Price of Freedom: War of Independence.**
7. **Thomas Edison's Light Bulb, 1879 (1 East) Lighting a Revolution.**
8. **John Bull Locomotive, 1831 (1 East).**
9. **Julia Child's Kitchen, 2001 (1 East)** You can practically hear Julia Child warbling about how to truss a chicken in this kitchen, with every pot in its pegboard place and marble countertops raised to suit her 6'2" stature.
10. **Abraham Lincoln's Top Hat (3 Center)** The American Presidency This is the top hat worn by Lincoln to Ford's Theatre on the night he was assassinated.

My appreciation for this museum is related to its origin. It opened as a small history and technology museum and has since expanded into one of the greatest places in D.C. The U.S. has a short artistic history compared to the rest of the world. On the other hand, U.S. merchandise and products manufactured in factories or laboratories represent a unique, American accomplishment. When it comes to innovation, the Museum of American History demonstrates how the U.S. leads the way.

Smithsonian National Museum of Natural History

10th Street & Constitution Avenue NW
10:00 a.m. - 5:30 p.m.
Metro: Smithsonian and Federal Triangle

On a sunny morning in June, I was once again in the long line of entry at the National Museum of Natural History. I'd gotten up early and made my way to the museum for an eagerly-awaited tour of D.C.'s reopened fossil and dinosaur hall. This hall, which has been under renovation for five years, will reignite public excitement for the museum and be a huge attraction.

The David H. Koch Hall of Fossils — Deep Time displays more than 700 specimens, including dinosaurs, plants, animals and insects, some never before displayed at the museum, while many previously on display have been reconditioned and reposed. Here, visitors can learn about the various creatures that have resided on Earth, from insects, birds, and mammals to marine organisms. Among the exhibit's many fossilized stars is a Tyrannosaurus rex, first discovered 30 years ago in Montana and on loan to the Smithsonian for 50 years. The museum also has the largest collections of vertebrate specimens, which trace the adaptations of mammals to their diverse and changing surroundings. Be sure to stop by the Insect Zoo to witness a live feeding of tarantulas!

Among one of the museum's many treats is the iconic 14-feet-tall, 12-ton stuffed African elephant, nicknamed Henry, which stands at the center of the rotunda. I recommend taking pictures of Henry to memorialize your visit.

If you are not a big fan of dinosaurs, insects, or stuffed elephants, the museum offers a bounty of other curiosities. The Smithsonian's National Gem and Mineral Collection stores approximately 35,000 meteorites, one of the most comprehensive collections of its kind in the world. If you plan to visit during the museum's busy season, like holidays or summer vacation, I recommend arriving at 10 a.m. or waiting until later in the day.

The 45.52-carat Hope diamond is the best known and largest blue diamond in the world.

National Zoo

3001 Connecticut Avenue NW
9:00 a.m. - 6:00 p.m. March 15 - September 30 (Grounds 8:00 a.m. - 7:00 p.m.)
9:00 a.m. - 4:00 p.m. October 1 - March 14 (Grounds 8:00 a.m. - 5:00 p.m.)
Metro: Woodley Park-Zoo/Adams Morgan Station

The National Zoo is a favorite for many families. It is home to hundreds of animals and offers plenty of great educational programming. There are comfortable benches and resting spots throughout the Zoo, which are conveniently placed for visitors who want to rest in-between visiting different exhibits.

Plan on spending at least a half day here. The Zoo is expansive, and it will take some time to explore the highlights and longer if you want to see more than just the popular exhibits. Arrive early if you drive. During peak times, most of the parking spaces are taken by 10:30 a.m. Even though admission is free, there is a $25 parking fee, so the best way to

get there is by public transportation. There are bus stops and Metro stations within walking distance of the Zoo.

The most popular animals in the Zoo are the pandas. They usually stay outside or inside the Giant Panda Habitat. The best time to see them is in the morning, which is when they spend time outside their enclosures. According to my friend who has volunteered for the zoo, pandas are solitary animals, so they are kept separately from each other.

Note that during peak visitation times, strollers may not be permitted inside animal buildings. On these days, designated stroller parking is provided by the main entrance to each building. Visitors can bring their own food and non-alcoholic drinks. Pets are not allowed in the zoo, with the exception of assistance animals.

Other Free Museums

National Gallery of Art

Constitution Avenue NW between 3rd and 9th Streets
Monday - Saturday: 10:00 a.m. - 5:00 p.m., Sunday: 11:00 a.m. - 6:00 p.m.
Metro: Archives-Navy Memorial, Judiciary Square, Smithsonian

If you are an architecture buff, I recommend adding the original Neoclassical West Building designed by John Russell Pope to your list of sights. The modern East Building offers a sharp contrast to the West. It was designed by I.M. Pei, whose work includes the famous Pyramid of Louvre in Paris.

East Building: After a three-year long renovation, the East Building now boasts two sky-lit tower galleries, which are close to staircases that connect all levels of the museum. The museum's gallery extends to the rooftop terrace where a dazzling blue rooster sculpture stands in the open air. Art pieces by Alexander Calder, Barbara Kruger, and Mark Rothko can be found here too, and they make

Leo Villareal *The Multiverse*, 2008

compelling reasons to climb to the top. Leo Villareal's incredible light sculpture, The Multiverse, connects the West and East building. Made of more than 41,000 LED nodes, they create abstract configurations that literally illuminate your way as you move from one building to the other via an underground concourse.

West Building: Gorgeous rooms await you in the West Building. The European sculpture gallery has more 900 pieces from the permanent collection, using natural light helping to authentically illuminate works from the medieval era.

Albert-Ernest Carrier-Belleuse
Fantasy Bust of A Veiled Woman
1865-1870

You need not rush to take pictures among the crowds at the National Gallery. There are comfortable benches, nice security guards who smile easily, and great paintings. You should also visit the Gallery's outdoor sculpture garden. A 6.1-acre space adjacent to the West building, the garden has beautiful trees and 17 sculptures taken from the Gallery's collection. Robert Indiana's famous AMOR, a play on the artist's LOVE series stands in a place of honor. The Pavilion Café, which offers year-round service, is a good place to take a break during a museum tour. The National Gallery of Art also hosts several events throughout the year, including concerts, guided tours, gallery talks and lectures. Check the museum's calendar before you go.

The following list includes some of my favorite things about this grand museum and I offer it as a guide:

Leonardo da Vinci
Ginevra de' Benci
c. 1474/1478

The subject of this painting, Ginevra de' Benci, was the daughter of a wealthy Florentine banker. Her portrait (the only painting by Leonardo da Vinci in the Americas) was probably commissioned around the time of Ginevra's marriage at age sixteen. It is among da Vinci's earliest experiments with oil paint and reveals the young artist as an innovator. Da Vinci daringly placed Ginevra in an open setting, in an era that was conservative. The three-quarter pose, which shows her steady reserve, is the first in Italian portraiture. On the reverse side of the painting, Da Vinci painted an emblem and the Latin motto: Virtem Forma Decorat ("Beauty adorns the virtue"). In the center is a juniper branch, which represents chastity, flanked on each side by laurel and palm, which imply artistic and literary inclinations and moral virtue respectively.

Vincent Van Gogh
Self-Portrait
Roses
c. 1889

Vincent Van Gogh painted himself a lot. Think of his numerous self-portraits like the selfies of his day. You should also check out the swirling brush stroke of Van Gogh's Roses. They make me feel like picking up some white flowers for myself.

Pablo Picasso
Family of Saltimbanques
c. 1905

We all know Pablo Picasso because of his famous Cubist technique. Those of you who are familiar with his history already understand that the Rose and Blue period represent the earlier stages of his career. This painting is one of his masterpieces from the Rose period.

Claude Monet
Woman with a Parasol - Madame Monet and Her Son
c. 1875

If I had an opportunity to take one of the masterpieces in the National Gallery of Art home with me, I would choose Claude Monet's Woman with a Parasol without any hesitation. Whenever I see this painting, I am convinced that Monet was a wonderful family guy as well as a great artist. His soft but strong brush stroke and skillful technique with light perfectly capture a loving moment between his wife and son. Through this painting, he shares his affection for his family with viewers. *Woman with a Parasol* represents the best the National Gallery of Art has to offer.

National Archives

Constitution Avenue NW between 7th & 9th Streets NW
10:00 a.m. - 5:30 p.m.
Metro: Archives

In front of the National Archives is a statue inscribed with the following words taken from Shakespeare's The Tempest: "What is past is prologue." These words have become a motto for the National Archives, which preserves documentary materials of the American experience. The museum is home to the Declaration of Independence, the Bill of Rights, the Constitution, and one of four extant copies of the Magna Carta. They are sealed in the most scientifically advanced housing that preservation technology can provide.

The National Archives is a must-see for history lovers and any visitor to D.C. No trip to the capital is complete without a stop. When you do visit, expect cool temperatures and low lighting within some areas of the building. Since light fades and destroys parchment and paper, the light levels in the Rotunda have to be kept low. Moreover, photography is prohibited to help preserve irreplaceable archival materials.

Library of Congress

101 Independence Avenue SE
Monday – Saturday: 8:30 a.m. – 4:30 p.m.
Metro: Capitol South

In this town, the early bird gets the worm. The Library of Congress opens earlier than the other museums in D.C. It provides reading rooms for visitors looking to conduct research and a free docent-led tour which is a great way to learn about the building's history and highlights.

In addition to the breathtaking architecture of the Library, its massive collection of books are worth stopping in to see. Some of them date back to the 1600s! The Library is the proud owner of a copy of the Gutenberg Bible, which was printed in the 1400s. Ongoing displays also include the map that first used the term "America" for the New World. Thomas Jefferson's own library is also a must see. Unlike the National Archives, photography is allowed in the public area of the Jefferson Building without flash.

If you want to use the Library's research areas, you must request a Reader Identification Card issued by the Library. It is free, and you can obtain one by registering with a valid driver's license, passport or state issued identification. Readers have to be 16 and above. The office is in the Madison Building Room LM 133 or the Jefferson Building Room LJ 139.

Bureau of Engraving and Printing

301 14th Street SW
Monday – Friday: 9:00 a.m. – 2:00 p.m.
Metro: Smithsonian

The Bureau of Engraving and Printing is sometimes confused with the U.S. Mint. Drop by for a guided tour and learn first-hand how the U.S. dollar is printed and protected from counterfeiting.

Tickets are free but sell out quickly. Arrive before 8 a.m. at the ticket booth located on Raoul Wallenberg Place SW (formerly 15th street) for a chance to claim a ticket. Keep in mind that taking photos is strictly forbidden inside this building.

I strongly recommend that you get your ticket and then take a walk around the Tidal Basin. I happened to visit during the cherry blossom season. Although the huge crowd interrupted my comfy stroll, I took some wonderful pictures.

White House Visitor Center

1450 Pennsylvania Avenue NW
7:30 a.m. - 4:00 p.m.
Metro: Federal Triangle

It is difficult to tour the White House, but the White House Visitor Center gives you a look at what America's most famous address is like on the inside. It provides a wealth of fascinating information and videos that will make you feel like you're actually there. Well, almost. It's a great stop to make if you're looking to learn more about U.S. presidential history.

U.S. Capitol Visitor Center

First Street NE
Monday – Saturday: 8:30 a.m. - 4:30 p.m.
Metro: Capitol South

If you're interested in a tour, you must schedule one in advance through the office of your Representative or Senator, or through the Capitol Building's online scheduling system. The Exhibition Hall provides great interactive displays about how the U.S government works.

The Capitol is indeed where laws are made in the United States, and it really makes an unforgettable impression on any visitor in D.C.

National Arboretum

3501 New York Avenue NW
8:00 a.m. - 5:00 p.m.
Metro: Stadium-Armory, Bus B2 to Bladensburg Road

The National Arboretum is quite a ways away from most other museums in D.C., but it is worth visiting. There are lovely gardens and wooded spots to stroll through. It is home to the Capitol Columns, which are the original columns from the U.S Capitol. The National Arboretum is one of my favorite places in the city where I visit at least once every season to appreciate its stunning beauty.

You should make some time to see the Bonsai garden and the Asian Collections. The Arboretum offers large parking lots, which is great because it is easier to get there by car than by public transportation.

United States Botanic Garden

100 Maryland Avenue SW
10:00 a.m. - 5:00 p.m.
Metro: Federal Center

The Botanic Garden is a perfect retreat from bustling city life. Brimming with flowers and trees, some of which are native to the rainforest, it offers every visitor a restful place to unwind. The holiday season is a particularly wonderful time to visit this garden, with model trains that run around, below, through and above plant -based recreations of iconic sights from across the United States. I was very glad to find most of well-known buildings in D.C. represented in a detailed manner here.

The DAR (Daughters of the American Revolution)

1775 D Street NW
Monday-Friday: 8:30 a.m. – 4:00 p.m.
Saturday: 9:00 a.m. – 5:00 p.m.

This treasured museum is located in the heart of D.C. I tried several times to visit, but something happened on an every occasion. Finally, I made it.

Although I assumed that I finished my museum list, I had to think seriously about if I would include this one.

A couple of months ago, I read an article in the newspaper that the'Daughters'had welcomed its first black woman to the national board. One notable woman who was a member of this organization was Eleanor Roosevelt, who gave up her membership in 1939 after the

DAR refused to allow a famous African American singer, Marian Anderson, to perform at its Constitution Hall.

Originally, The DAR was open to women who could show that they were descendants of the Rebel Army of the American Revolutionary War, fought between the Battle of Lexington in 1775, and the withdrawal of British troops in 1783.

I was mesmerized by the white historic building, many artifacts spread between 2 galleries, and period rooms where I could see many different lifestyles in the history of the American home. Depending on specific topics, each room offers more detailed explanations and displays. For example, you can find a Kentucky room which was inspired

by Ancient Greek and Roman architecture, and a New Hampshire room where a lot of toys are displayed in the attic.

Lastly, you can't miss an elegant library located in the center of this building.

I really recommend this wonderful place to those who are interested in American history and children who love dollhouses.

Art Museum of the Americas

201 18th Street NW
Tuesday – Sunday: 10:00 a.m. - 5:00 p.m.

Located in a perfect area in D.C, the Art Museum of the Americas is primarily devoted to exhibiting works of contemporary art from Latin America and the Caribbean. It was formally established by the Organization of American States in 1976. The first permanent collection housed 250 artworks, expanding over the next quarter-century to over 2000 items of fascinating paintings, photographs, installations, drawings, and sculptures from the early 20th century and onwards. In addition to its main collection of Caribbean and Latin American art, the AMA hosts temporary and special exhibitions from across the region, and provides educational seminars and lectures from the invited speakers. It is a quiet place to relax with awesome art pieces.

I attended a cocktail party here once, which was held on the terrace and I was duly impressed by the setting. I felt as if I was in a scene from "The Great Gatsby." The museum provides a calendar of special events that is available on its website.

United States Holocaust Memorial Museum

100 Raoul Wallenberg Pl SW
10:00 a.m. - 5:30 p.m.
Metro: Smithsonian

Many museums are places where you go to have some fun. But it is critically important that we learn about and remember some of the most horrible incidents in history so that they are never repeated. The United States Holocaust Memorial Museum educates the public about the Holocaust in a sensitive and honest manner. This museum is not likely to be your favorite, but it will probably be the most memorable and impactful of the D.C museums that you visit.

The centerpiece of the United States Holocaust Memorial Museum is the permanent exhibition, simply titled "The Holocaust." Spread across three floors, the exhibit uses artifacts, photographs and films to narrate the history of tragedy chronologically. It also includes personal objects that belonged to survivors and audio testimonies from eyewitnesses. Another powerful exhibit presents the history of the Holocaust through the experience of a child named Daniel. On every Wednesday and Thursday morning from mid-March to mid-August at 11 a.m., survivors arrive at the museum to share their stories about the Holocaust.

The Holocaust Museum is a place of and for reflection on our past.

Therefore, when you arrive at the Hall of Remembrance on the second floor, light a candle and quietly reflect on all that you've learned. Lastly, if you want further information about this horrific incident, resources on the website are very helpful.

Tickets are required to visit the museum from March to August.

Glenstone Museum

12100 Glen Road, Potomac MD
Thursday – Sunday: 10:00 a.m. - 5:00 p.m.

The Glenstone Museum is a place that seamlessly integrates art, architecture, and landscape into a serene environment. Most museums put an emphasis on the collection inside the building. However, the Glenstone is extraordinary not only for what's inside but also because of its outdoor space, which is designed to facilitate meaningful encounters for visitors. I have visited this gorgeous place several times, and I am always mesmerized by the state of mind that the Glenstone creates by the energy of its architecture, the power of the artworks, and the restorative qualities of nature. The name Glenstone derives from two local sources: Glen Road, where the property line begins, and a type of carderock stone indigenous to the area, which is still extracted from nearby quarries.

Glenstone offers nearly 300 acres of landscape fully integrated with architecture and contemporary artworks. The museum's breathtaking landscape includes paths, trails, streams, meadows, forests, and seventeen outdoor sculptures scattered throughout the grounds. The newly built pavilions offer abundant collections which enhance the pleasure of visiting this place.

Outdoor sculptures are installed throughout the expansive grounds. Contour, made by Richard Serra, and Jeff Koons's 37-foot tall flower-draped Split-Rocker are notable items in the collection. My son ridiculously mistook the Felix Gonzalez-Torres's Untitled for a bench, and he tried to sit on it. What happened? His pants were completely soaked in water. A museum worker said that it was a common accident.

Photography is not permitted inside the museum. When I asked why, the museum worker said that it would distract from the experience of other visitors as well as our own experience by interfering with our focus on the objects themselves. This is really true. I often make the mistake of not concentrating on the direct interaction between me and the paintings. Instead, I waste my time taking braggy pictures to appease my vanity.

You have to make a reservation for entry, as there are a limited number of visitors permitted. The most impressive thing about this museum is that I sent an email to a person involved during the weekend to ask if I could get a ticket. Because all were sold out until May, I explained my special situation: I am writing a guidebook about D.C. museums. Fortunately, I got a very rapid and kind answer from her. Thanks to her hospitality, this wonderful museum grows on me more.

Right bottom: Felix Gonzalez-Torres *Untitled*, 1992-1995

Octagon Museum

1799 New York Avenue NW
Thursday – Saturday: 1:00 p.m. - 4:00 p.m.
Metro: Farragut West

Designed by Dr. William Thornton, the first architect of the United States Capitol, the Octagon House originally served as the winter home of the prominent Tayloe family, but has also been a tenement apartment building, a girls' school and the headquarters of the American Institute of Architects. It was completed in 1801 and is now open as a museum administered by the American Institute of Architects Foundation. This place interprets life in early Washington, D.C., the history of architecture, and the role of architectural design in our lives. Strange to say, the house has 6 sides, but it was called "the Octagon" by the Tayloes, the original owners of the mansion.

Built of brick trimmed with Aquia Creek sandstone, the Octagon House looks very elegant and beautiful. It was ahead of its time with closets on every floor.

The Octagon Museum is also a historic place, because after the burning of the White House by the British, President Madison ratified the Treaty of Ghent that ended the War of 1812, in one of the upstairs rooms. There's a funny corollary to this story, which is that the owner of the Octagon House was a Federalist and didn't support President Madison politically. He is said to have received $500 in rent for the Madison's six-month residency in the building.

It's 1814 . . .
Do you know where your President is?
THE OCTAGON served as the temporary White House for President Madison and his family after the British burned Washington during the War of 1812.
Tour this piece of lesser-known history today.
The Octagon Museum
FREE AND OPEN TO THE PUBLIC
THURS-SAT, 1-4 p.m.
1799 New York Ave, NW

Dumbarton Oaks Museum

1803 32nd Street NW
Tuesday – Sunday: 11:30 a.m. - 5:30 p.m.
Museum admission is free, Garden Admission is $10

Dumbarton Oaks is a historic estate in the Georgetown neighborhood which was the residence and garden of Robert Wood Bliss and his wife Mildred Barnes Bliss. Its Research Library and Collection was founded here by the Bliss couple who gave the property to Harvard University in 1940. The research institute is dedicated to supporting scholarship in the fields of Byzantine and Pre Columbian studies, as well as garden design and landscape architecture.

The Byzantine Collection comprises more than 1200 objects from the fourth to the fifteenth centuries. In addition to its Byzantine holdings, the collection includes Greek, Roman and western medieval artworks and objects from the ancient Near East, Ptolemaic Egypt, and various Islamic cultures.

Principal to the collection is the renaissance-style Music room which features displays of tapestries, sculptures, paintings and furnishings dating from the fifteenth to the eighteenth centuries. The Bliss used this room for hosting musical programs and scholarly lectures, and it continues to serve these purposes.

Note: Dumbarton Oaks Museum is different from Dumbarton House, owned by The National Society of Colonial Dames of America. Dumbarton House is located on 2715 Q street. Built in 1799, this small house museum offers guests a unique opportunity to view one of the finest examples of Federal period architecture in the U.S, along with its impressive collection of furniture and decorative arts.

EXIT

Folger Shakespeare Library

201 E Capitol Street SE
Monday – Saturday: 10:00 a.m. - 5:00 p.m., Sunday: Noon - 5:00 p.m.

This Capitol Hill institution houses the largest collection of Shakespeare artifacts in the world, as well as manuscripts, books, and arts from the Renaissance era. It is an ideal place to visit for educators, students, and literary buffs.

The Folger is an internationally recognized research library, which offers advanced scholarly programs in the humanities. Free docent-led tours are provided daily. When I visited on a Sunday, I was mesmerized by the beauty of the reading room and its collection.

The docent was Nicole who was a former librarian of a historic library. She was passionate and knowledgeable about this collection. Before you go, check their website to confirm that it's not closed for renovation.

Anderson House

2118 Massachusetts Avenue NW
Tuesday – Saturday: 10:00 a.m. - 4:00 p.m., Sunday: Noon - 4:00 p.m.

Explore the Society of the Cincinnati's historic headquarters, a National Historic Landmark that has been the Society's home since 1938. I happened to see this gorgeous mansion on my way to the Phillips Collection. Later, I took a tour of the mansion, which was very interesting to me, because I'd been in the middle of a biography on Alexander Hamilton, who had been a member of the Society. The estate, first owned by American diplomat Larz Anderson in 1905, works to preserve the history of the American Revolution. Surprisingly, the Anderson's art collection features many works from Asia.

Society of the Cincinnati Medal Badge, 1783

Old Korean Legation Museum

1500 13th Street NW
Tuesday – Sunday: 10:00 a.m. - 5:00 p.m.

As I was taking a walk in the historic Logan Circle neighborhood, an elegant building catches my eye. It was the Old Korean Legation Museum, established in 1877. After becoming official in 1889, the building was an important stage for the diplomatic wing of the Joseon dynasty and the Korean Empire at large. However, the Old Korean Legation had to end due to the Korea-Japan annexation. Repurchase by the Cultural Heritage Administration for $3.5 million in 2012 enabled the building to be renovated. Today, the Old Korean Legation Museum is an immaculate example of nineteenth-century architecture in D.C. and highly valued for its historical significance.

As soon as you enter, you can find the Korean flag replicated in its original form. This 3-story building features special rooms designed for public and private purposes. Many artifacts based on historical photos and documents are meticulously recreated. The most impressive item is a photograph of a young boy. He was the son of a diplomatic minister, who became one of the members of a patriotic group. Lastly, explore a small but well maintained garden with several traditional touchs. Decorated with red bricks and tiles that depict four Korean plants: bamboo, plum blossom, orchid , and chrysanthemum, this is a must see.

The Old Legation Building is available for tours in Korean as well as in English. Be sure you remove your shoes when entering. Otherwise, guests are given covers for their footwear.

Museums with a Fee or Recommended Donation

Phillips Collection

1600 21st Street NW
Tuesday – Saturday: 10:00 a.m. - 5:00 p.m. (extended hours until 8:30 p.m. on Thursdays), Sundays: Noon - 6:00 p.m.
Metro: Dupont Circle
Access to the permanent collection is free, but special exhibitions cost $12

If you are a big fan of Pierre-Auguste Renoir, you must not miss the Phillips Collection. Renoir's Luncheon of the Boating Party is probably one of the most famous paintings here. Moreover, as a big fan of Mark Rothko, I am very delighted to sit on a bench in deep meditation in the Rothko Room, the first public space dedicated solely to the artist's works. The room was designed by the Phillips in keeping with Rothko's expressed preference for exhibiting his large, luminous paintings in small but intimate spaces.

Regardless of its small size, the Phillips Collection is a wonderful place to come to for high end culture. The Sunday concerts, one of the longest running music series in the area, features extraordinary musicians and is regarded as one of the best cultural events in D.C. The series runs on Sundays from October through May. Performers range from established and well-known artists to promising new musicians.

RightTop: Pierre-Auguste Renoir, *Luncheon of the Boating Party*, 1880-1881, The Phillips Collections, Acquired 1923,

Right Below: The Rothko Room, Mark Rothko

The President Woodrow Wilson House

2340 S Street NW
Tuesday and Sunday: Noon - 4:00 p.m., Wednesday – Saturday: 10:00 a.m. - 4:00 p.m.
Cost: $10 for adults, $8 for seniors 62 and older, $5 for students, free for children 12 and under.

The Woodrow Wilson house was the residence of the 28th President after he left office. The house contains some elaborate items from the Wilson White House and retains the style and aesthetic of American homes in the 1920s. Wilson purchased this house in the last month of his second term of the presidency. It features a marble entryway and a grand staircase.

It was from the balcony of this house that Wilson addressed a crowd on November 11, 1923 in his final public appearance. On February 3,1924 Wilson passed away in an upstairs bedroom and was buried in the National Cathedral. The National Trust for Historic Preservation owns the house and operates it as a museum.

Kreeger Museum

2401 Foxhall Road NW
Tuesday – Saturday: 10:00 a.m. - 4:00 p.m.
Metro: Tenleytown-AU
Cost: Suggested donation of $10

This private museum offers an opportunity to check out artworks you won't find anywhere else in D.C. – and certainly not in any of the major galleries or museums. The Kreeger provides an intimate viewing experience away from the crowds. Picasso, Renoir, Monet and Sisley are some of the highlights of the Kreeger collection. Top off the experience with a short stroll through its cozy garden, where you'll find some spectacular sculptures.

What amazes me the most about the Kreeger is the building itself. This jewel-box house museum was designed by Philip Johnson, who

also designed the pavilion for Dumbarton Oaks, in 1963. Both buildings marked a transitional moment in Johnson's shift from International Style severity to Post-modernist pomp. Built with hand-crafted travertine, the Kreeger is expressed through a series of cube-shaped galleries, each one capped by ribbed ceiling vaults. From the outside, the building looks like a linked modular dome.

A reservation is recommended prior to visiting. Otherwise, you are going to be frustrated when you find the door closed to you on arrival.

Arshile Gorky *Untitled*, 1936-1937

President Lincoln's Cottage

140 Rock Creek Church Rd NW
9:30 a.m. – 4:30 p.m.
Cost: $15 for adults, $5 for children (6-12) and $12 for Military (must present valid ID)

A retreat from the White House, President Lincoln's Cottage was the home where Abraham Lincoln spent summers with his family and first developed the Emancipation Proclamation. Today, the Gothic Revival-style cottage hosts public and private tours. I was surprised that there was a huge space preserved for President Lincoln near the White House. A very detailed explanation from a tour guide helped me realize that the Cottage was the home for many brave ideas.

Hillwood Estate Museum

4155 Linnean Avenue NW
Tuesday – Sunday: 10:00 a.m. - 5:00 p.m.
Cost: $18 when you reserve online, $15 for Seniors and Students

Hillwood Estate Museum & Gardens is a decorative arts museum. It was once the residence of a businesswoman, Marjorie Merriweather Post. She was heir to the Postum Cereal Company, which became General Foods. She exerted a strong hand in the business affairs of her company long before women appeared in major corporate boardrooms.

In 1977 Hillwood opened to the public, introducing the world to a comprehensive collection of Russian imperial art, a large decorative arts collection that focuses heavily on the House of Romanov, an assortment of Fabergé eggs, a distinguished collection of French art

from the 1700s, and twenty-five acres of landscaped gardens and natural woodlands.

There are beautiful gardens with themed areas like French parterre, the Rose Garden, a Japanese-style garden, a pet cemetery, the Lunar Lawn, and the Friendship Walk.

The Mansion tour features exquisite furnishings and historic objects. When you enter the house, you're greeted by the large portrait of Empress Catherine the Second who ruled Russia from 1762 to 1796. She is credited with westernizing and modernizing Russia. Be sure not to miss the Imperial Easter Eggs by Fabergé which were gifts from Russia's last tsar to his mother, Maria Feodorovna.

National Building Museum

401 F Street NW
Monday – Saturday: 10:00 a.m. - 5:00 p.m., Sunday: 11:00 a.m. - 5:00 p.m
Metro: Judiciary Square
Cost: $10 for adults, discounted tickets for seniors, children, and students

The National Building Museum is beautiful and worth exploring on its own. There are many educational and hands-on exhibits which could be interesting to your kids. Check out the special exhibits for which this Museum is famous before visiting.

National Geographic Museum

145 17th Street NW
10:00 a.m. - 6:00 p.m.
Metro: Farragut West or Farragut North
Cost: $15 for adults, discounted tickets for seniors, children, and students

If you want to explore the world in a single museum, the National Geographic Museum is the right place to go. Known for its stunning photographs and rotating exhibits, this museum is a favorite for families.

Much of the space is dedicated to current exhibitions. If you are planning to visit, take a look at what's currently on display before committing to paying the ticket price. One impressive room is simply a display of all the covers of National Geographic magazine.

National Museum of Women in the Arts

New York Avenue and 13th Street NW
Monday – Saturday: 10:00 a.m. - 5:00 p.m., Sunday: Noon - 5:00 p.m.
Metro: Metro Center
Cost: adults $10, discounted tickets for seniors, children, and students

Explore some of the most impressive artworks by female artists. Paintings by Frida Kahlo and Georgia O'Keefe are definite highlights in the National Museum of Women in the Arts. But don't overlook the incredible talents of lesser-known and contemporary artists who are working in a range of mediums, from paintings to sculptures.

The George Washington University Museum and the Textile Museum

701 21 Street NW
Mondays & Fridays: 11:00 a.m. - 5:00 p.m., Wednesdays & Thursdays: 11 a.m. - 7:00 p.m., Saturday: 10:00 a.m. - 5:00 p.m., Sunday: 1:00 p.m. - 5:00 p.m.
Cost: $8 suggested donation
Metro: Foggy-Bottom

Located on the George Washington University campus, the Textile Museum, which opened in 1925, has an enormous collection of more than 20,000 textiles and other objects, showcasing the cultural importance of textiles from all over the world. I visited on a quiet, rainy Saturday morning, which was a perfect time for hanging out in a museum. You can find a parking spot close by. I recommend purchasing unique crafts (at reasonable prices) in the museum shop. The best thing for me is to revisit that feeling of freshness that comes with being in a university again. It brings me back to my school days.

Albert H. Small
Washingtoniana
Collection
GW
MUSEUM
SHOP
SALE

Newseum

555 Pennsylvania Avenue NW
Monday – Saturday: 9:00 a.m. – 5:00 p.m., Sunday: 10:00 a.m. – 5:00 p.m.
Metro: Archives/Navy Memorial/Penn Quarter
Cost: adults $24.95+tax, discounted tickets for seniors and children under 18

The Newseum is worth the price of admission. When visitors enter at the concourse level, they will find the Newseum's signature video, "What's News". If you have limited time but lots of interest, take a 60-minute-long First Amendment Highlights Tour of the Newseum and explore the very best of its exhibits and collections.

If you have plenty of time, the folks at the Newseum recommend that guests proceed from the concourse up to the sixth floor via a glass elevator. On this topmost level is one of the museum's must-see attractions: the Greenspun Terrace, which offers you wonderful panoramic views of D.C.

Video clips and artifacts comprise exhibits on historical events from the past few decades. On display in a special gallery commemorating 9/11 is the twisted wreckage of the broadcast Antenna from the World Trade Center and front pages of newspapers from all around the world of that tragic day.

Take some time to look at the section of the Berlin Wall on display and learn how the concrete wall couldn't stop the free flow of information that eventually liberated East Germany.

As you know, news is the first draft of history. You can see all the front pages of significant historical events in the history gallery. There is also a Pulitzer Prize Winning Photographs Gallery and an I-Witness 4-D Adventure theatre in the museum.

Save on your admission by asking about discounts, which are available to AAA members and students with ID. It's also possible to save money by booking tickets online.

Note: The Newseum will be closing its current location on December 31, 2019 due to the building's sale to Johns Hopkins University. The Freedom Forum said that they will explore all options to find a new home in the D.C. area.

SPY
SPY MUSEUM STORE

International Spy Museum

700 L'Enfant Plaza SW
Monday – Saturday: 9:00 a.m. - 7:00 p.m., Sunday: 10:00 a.m. - 7:00 p.m.
Metro: Smithsonian
cost: $14-21

If you love James Bond or the Bourne series, the International Spy Museum should be your next destination. Recently, it moved and expanded its size and collection. The new 140,000-square foot building features exhibits and collections that reveal intelligence secrets and explore issues from today's headlines such as disinformation, cyber security, terrorism, surveillance and more.

New exhibits showcase the variety of ways technology is transforming the espionage craft. They turn a spotlight on intelligence failures and successes throughout history that have shaped our world. The museum's staff and Advisory Board include top ranked members of the intelligence community and experts in the field who draw on their decades of experience and first-hand knowledge to develop the museum's exhibits and programs.

This museum is a private non-profit dedicated to understanding tradecraft, history and the contemporary role of espionage, featuring the largest collection currently on public display. Moreover, this Museum dives into the alluring pop culture world of spies that the public knows well, but it digs much deeper to explore and demystify the real intelligence work which is often stranger than fiction.

Madame Tussauds Washington, D.C.

1001 F St NW
Monday – Saturday: 10:00 a.m. - 6:00 p.m., Sunday: 10:00 a.m. - 5:00 p.m.
Metro: Metro Center
Cost: adults $19.50, children $15.25

This interesting place allows visitors to interact with celebrities and historical figures through an extensive collection of lifelike wax figures. Hang out and pose for photos with some of your favorite athletes, singers and historical figures across uniquely themed rooms. The Presidents Gallery is one of the main attractions. Take a seat at the Resolute desk in the Oval Office, as if you were the President of the United States.

I was so thrilled to meet a wax figure of current President, Donald Trump and took a picture with it. Unlike many of the museums in D.C., Madame Tussauds has an entry fee, but there are ways to save your money. You can get discounted tickets if you buy them online.

Tips for Planning a Museum Tour

1. **For museums that require tickets, purchase them online ahead of time**

   For most large museums that require tickets, you can get them online in advance. You'll avoid the hassle of long lines in bad weather. Online tickets are sometimes cheaper as well.

2. **Know the free/discount days**

   If you're under budgetary constraints for a costly museum visit, be sure to search for a free or discounted tickets for specific occasions. Fortunately, every Smithsonian museum is free for entry.

3. **Avoid peak times if you can.**

   Nobody wants to wander around in a crowded museum. Get to a museum at opening or a few hours before closing time.

4. **Plan as many details that you can**

   Most museums–even smaller ones–have their own websites that will help you plan your visit down to the last detail.

5. **Consider guided tours, programs, and classes**

   Well-known museums have professional volunteers as tour guides who are on-hand to answer your questions and guide you on a tour that will enhance your experience of the museum. There are also classes and other interactive programs led by knowledgeable guides that provide a wealth of context and narrative.

6. **Don't stay the entire day**

   Even though I am a crazy museum lover, after a couple of hours in a museum, my legs get tired, and my brain starts to fog. There's a real name for this phenomenon: museum fatigue. According to some articles, as the length of a museum visit increases, the visitor's engagement decreases.

7. **Make a visit as interactive as possible**

   Museums provide many interactive programs for visitors, and actual participation in activities will more easily create lasting memories of your visit.

8. **Consider buying something at the gift store**

   Spending some money in the museum store is my indulgence. Since their products are often aesthetically beautiful, I set time aside to buy some souvenirs. When my kids were younger, I lured them to museums by permitting them to grab some toys in the museum store after a visit. Although toys usually were left unattended after my sons unpacked their suitcases, some artifacts remained close to us for a long time.

9. **Continue the discussion at home**

   The main reason of going to a museum is to learn something new and to expand your mind. You can reflect on the experience and talk about it with other folks including your kids and spouse, which makes the experience that much richer.

Tips on Smithsonian Museums for kids

Since Smithsonian Museums are free, you can leave without feeling guilty after a short visit. Here are some special programs for kids:

1. Smithsonian Sleepovers

Imagine rolling out your sleeping bag beneath a 50-foot whale, at the home of the Star - Spangled Banner, in the shadow of the space shuttle Discovery, or beside portraits of presidents and visionaries. These museums offer a night of fun that features tours, games, crafts, and more. Only one night out changed my kid, and I found a grown-up the next morning.

Participating museums include:

- Udvar-Hazy Center
- American History Museum
- Natural History Museum
- National Portrait Gallery

2. American History Museum

The Lemelson Center for the Study of Invention and Innovation invites children between the ages of 6-12 to create, collaborate, explore, and experiment. Spark! Lab activities for kids and families are also designed to connect common themes from daily life with the Museum's exhibits. Wegmans Wonderplace welcomes curious kids aged 6 and under, accompanied by an adult, to exercise their imaginations, wiggle their bodies, and explore with their hands. This place is the first exhibition on the National Mall designed for children. It is open from 10:00 a.m. to 4:00 p.m. daily except Tuesdays and Christmas.

3. Air and Space Museum

The Udvar-Hazy Center near Dulles International Airport has the Observation Tower, where you can watch real planes take off and land very closely. You can also ride flight simulators for an additional fee. There's an IMAX theatre too.

The main Museum in the mall has a "How Things Fly" exhibit that is the best place to start with younger children. This hands-on exhibit allows participants to touch and sit in an airplane, push buttons and find out how these massive vehicles fly in the sky. Because the museum offers daily programs involving science, kids are always welcome to make and fly their own paper airplane, look through a real telescope with astronomy experts, and take in a show at the Planetarium.

4. Freer and Sackler Gallery of Art

ImaginiAsia Family Programs

Open studio: All aged with adult companions,

Art & Me Workshops: Ages 3-5 with adult companions

Family Workshops: Ages 6-12 with adult companions

Teen Workshops: Ages 9-13 without adult companions

Family Festival

Summer Art Camps: Ages 7-12

5. National Zoo

Highlights include Tiger Tracks, Amazonia Science Gallery, Reptile Discovery Center, Kids' Farm and the Conservation Carousel.

6. Postal Museum

Meet Owney, the mascot dog of the Railway Post Office. Here kids can create a stamp using their own design, write and mail a postcard, sit in the cab of postal truck, ride in a stagecoach and sort packages like folks in the mail room. Check out the museum's kid-friendly itinerary before you embark.

7. Natural History Museum

Highlights include the Insect Zoo, Q?rius jr., the Discovery Room, and Live Butterflies.

Q?rius is an experimental and interactive learning space for tweens and teens allowing them to engage in real life science experiments.

Open daily, 10:00 a.m. - 5:00 p.m., ground floor

8. American Indian Museum

At the ImagiNation Activity Center, kids can explore ancient cultures by playing percussion instruments and stepping inside a traditional native home. In addition, family storytelling activities take place every Sunday morning.

9. Library of Congress

The Young Readers Center (Room LJ-G29) welcomes children and teens to read books or participate in various activities.

Mondays – Saturdays: 10:00 a.m. - 4:00 p.m.

Paying Museum Programs for Kids

International Spy Museum

Not only is there lots of new stuff to see, but you can participate in an Undercover Mission and discover numerous hands-on elements at this newly built museum.

The Newseum

Kids adore becoming a television reporter at the Newseum. Kids can read from a teleprompter and take part in the NBC Interactive Newsroom, all the while learning about the value of truth.

Tips for Seniors and People with Disabilities

Washington D.C. is one of the most accessible cities for people with special needs. Visiting museums might be a burdensome task to someone. Museums are really intimidating, aren't they? Fortunately, all of D.C.'s attractions and cultural institutions maintain dedicated web pages outlining their accessibility features, including ramps, ASL tours, and wheelchairs. There are also several programs in the city intended to ensure that on-street parking is available to both residents and visitors with disabilities. Metro is proud of being one of the most accessible public transportation systems in the world. Metro has compiled a downloadable guide to accessible transportation options throughout the region. (https://www.wmata.com)

1. Visit a museum that has a specific focus, rather than a general interest one. For example, Dumbarton Oaks is an excellent choice for those intrigued by Byzantine icons.

2. Make use of time and energy-saving equipment, such as free manual wheelchair loans available at every museum in Washington D.C and at the Zoo on a first come, first serve basis. If you want a special tour, you will have to pre-arrange them. For questions about disability programs, call (202) 633-2921.

3. Enter the National Museum of Natural History via the Constitution avenue entrance. (This is the side opposite the National Mall entrance, which isn't wheelchair accessible.) In addition, if you need companion care restrooms, they are located on the first-floor Rotunda near the Ocean Hall.

4. When it comes to the Air and Space museum, don't jump to the conclusion that you won't be able to feel a thrill in the super-large IMAX theatre. Of course, you can be provided with accessible entrances, restrooms, and a parking space. If you need to rent a wheelchair at the museum, use the Independence Avenue entrance and talk to the friendly folks at the Security desk.

5. All of the stunning exhibits at the National Museum of the American Indian are wheelchair accessible and can be accessed by elevator. Both entrances to the museum feature ramps. There's parking available at the northeast corner of Jefferson Drive and 4th Street SW.

6. The National Gallery of Art is equipped with accessible parking, wheelchairs, and ramps. In case you're having a hard time locating parking, the officer stationed outside the West Building at the 4th Street plaza can help. Take advantage of the benches in the museums. Sit down frequently, not because you are tired but because you'll be able to appreciate a master's spirit completely. Resting your feet is just a bonus

Checklist When You plan to Go to Museums with the Elderly

When you are accompanying the elderly to museums, you have to be more careful to treat them appropriately, so not to turn a wonderful museum visit into an unpleasant experiences due to some trivial mistake. The two most basic things that you have to keep in mind are, (1) remain mindful of their condition and (2) know what to expect at your intended destination. Although you may feel you are fully aware of your parent's current health condition, interest, and financial state, they could be hiding something as so not to bother you. For example, if your mother has diabetes, she may have hypoglycemia in the middle of museum tour.

☐ How long does it take to get there?

If it's more than 90 minutes, make sure you plan a restroom stop along the way. It's also a good idea to bring enough non-perishable snacks and bottled water on the trip.

☐ What is the price of admission?

Although there are senior discounted rates for admission, it may not be enough for those facing financial hardship. Fortunately, most museums in D.C. area are free. But some museums, like the Newseum, the International Spy Museum, and Hillwood Estate have an admission fee. Don't forget to bring an identification card to prove age.

☐ Are there stairs? How many and how steep?

Unless famous historic estates are equipped with an elevator, or any facility to help people with special care, just forget about it. You will experience hell.

☐ Is the museum well lit?

Many seniors face deteriorating vision as they age, and dark interior spaces can increase the risk of injury for those with low vision. Bumping into furniture or tripping over a rug due to poor lighting is very common and can lead to a big accident.

☐ Are outdoor paths and walkways fairly flat?

Uneven walkways can cause problems for anyone, but especially for seniors. As people age, their ability to balance and avoid hazards becomes slow and poor. A fall that is merely an embarrassing thing to someone younger could be truly life threatening for an older adult.

☐ If the tour is guided, how long is it and what is the approximate distance that will be covered?

Though many active seniors can walk long distances, most of them cannot. No matter how fascinating a story the docent is telling, standing for long periods of time can be intolerable. In some cases, the elderly have hearing problems and can't catch the docent's fast or unclear explanations. Talk to your docent early on about any special needs they may have to accommodate.

☐ Are the labels that identify and explain each exhibit legible to people with low vision?

Audio headsets are increasingly common in larger museums, which can be a huge help.

☐ Are restrooms easily accessible?

Although this is important for museum goers of all ages, it is especially critical for older adults who may have medical conditions or be taking medications with side effects including frequent and urgent visits to restroom. Lastly, make sure to ask if they are only accessible by stairs or if they can be reached by ramp or elevator. Also find out if there are enough stalls to accommodate several people at a time.

Hoon's Pick

1. For the Beginner

Target the major Museums in D.C. There are tons of things to see and feel in there. Pick one among them. You will never regret it.

1. National Museum of Natural History
2. National Air & Space Museum
3. National Museum of American History
4. National Gallery of Art
5. National Museum of African American History and Culture
6. National Archives

2. For the Intermediate Challenger

Expand your knowledge and delve into the collections that interest you. I divide these visitors into groups based on their interests:

1. For Art Lovers

- **a.** National Portrait Gallery and Smithsonian American Art Museum
- **b.** Phillips Collection
- **c.** Hirshhorn Museum
- **d.** Renwick Gallery

2. For History Buffs

- **a.** U.S Capitol & Capitol Visitors Center
- **b.** United States Holocaust Museum
- **c.** National Postal Museum
- **d.** President Lincoln's cottage
- **e.** U.S Bureau of Engraving & Printing

3. For Science Geeks

a. International Spy Museum

b. National Air & Space Museum of Steven F. Udvar-Hazy Center

c. National Building Museum

d. National Geographic Museum

4. For Nature Roamers

a. Hillwood Estate Museum

b. National Arboretum

c. Botanic Garden

3. For the Advanced Explorer

Connect these new places with your previous visits. They will build up an extensive network of knowledge and experience.

1. For Art Lovers

Dumbarton Oaks Museum, Kreeger Museum, Art Museum of the Americas, and the Glenstone Museum are on the list.

2. For History Buffs

Anderson Mansion, Octagon Museum, Woodrow Wilson's House and Library of Congress are perfect sites to satisfy your curiosity.

3. For Science Geeks

The National Cryptologic Museum, the United States Botanic Garden, and the National Museum of Health and Medicine are waiting for your visit.

4. For 1-day Itinerary

Choose one or two museums out of the many listed above. It is up to your interests, situation, experience, season, and established knowledge about museums.

5. For 2-day Itinerary

Pick two to four museums as suited to your physical condition. One half or two-thirds of your list should be for major museums and the rest should be a small but unique one off the National Mall.

6. For 3-day Itinerary

Make a list that features at least one outdoor museum and one history related museum, because there are so many awesome places in D.C. I believe that history museums in D.C. are not only ingenious but also very interesting. Honestly, you can find better art museums in other cities such as London, Paris, and New York, but there are several museums that only exist in D.C.

7. For 4-day Itinerary

If you are able to afford the entry fees, the Newseum, Madame Tussauds Wax Museum, the International Spy Museum, and ARTECHOUSE all close late in the evening and are perfect late-night attractions in D.C., so you can use your time economically.

8. For 5-day Itinerary

Deep, Deeper and the Deepest. Five days is quite a long period to focus on your genuine interests. You can be immersed in the magnificent collection of each museum you choose as long as you want to stay.

Sample Museum Trips

Plan for 1-day Itinerary

Route: National Zoo

Visitors: Michael, a 35- year- old male Virginia resident, his wife, and their 3-month-old baby.

To celebrate his wife's birthday, Mike planned to give her a present. However, since his wife wanted to have a casual family trip, he thought of the National Zoo. He heard that the weekend is hectic with visitors, so he decided to take paternal leave on a weekday. He and his wife are so thrilled by their first family event. It is almost eleven when they arrive at the Zoo. Since there is rarely any available parking spaces, Mike has no choice but to drive around for quite some time until a space is open. The parking fee is a flat $25. There are already many kids inside the Zoo. Young parents with babies in strollers are commonly found. When Mike and his family finally enter the Zoo, they go to the upper area to meet the famous panda and watch it eat bamboo leaves, which looks very peaceful. At last, he takes a family photo in front of the Zoo.

Plan for 2-day Itinerary

Route: Library of Congress, Capitol Visitor Center, United States Botanic Garden, National Museum of the American Indian, National Gallery of Art, The White House, Renwick Gallery, Freer-Sackler Museum, Smithsonian Castle

Visitor: Linda, a 40-year-old, physically fit, single female. Linda travels a lot and is an art lover.

Early in the morning, Linda goes to the Library of Congress via Metro from her hotel. She takes a guided tour that includes the Reading Room and President Jefferson's library. It's only 10:00 a.m. when Linda gets out of the library. The weather is perfect, so she decides to take a walk. She goes to see the exotic trees and flowers in the Botanic Garden, but then realizes that she is hungry. There aren't any good restaurants near the National Mall. She remembers that there is a wonderful cafeteria in the National Museum of the American Indian. Fortunately, that museum is very close to the Botanic Garden. As soon as she reaches the Museum cafeteria, Mitsitam, she orders Pueblo tacos which taste delicious. Her energy is restored and she is ready to explore the museum.

When her first mission is done in the American Indian Museum, the hands of her watch point to 2:45 p.m. Although her feet hurt a little, she is still hungry for museums. She is torn between going to the National Air and Space Museum and appreciating the 20th American paintings in the National Gallery of Art. Even though the Air and Space Museum is located right next to the American Indian Museum, it is very crowded with elementary students getting on the bus at the museum's entrance. She decides to spend the late afternoon in the East Building of the National Art Gallery. The newly built East Building is so cool and instead of rushing, she walks slowly along the paintings which draw her eyes and touch her heart. Last summer, she had been to Paris to see an exhibit on Impressionism. Today, she focuses on the Abstract Expressionist and Cubist artworks housed in the East Building. She climbs the tower where her favorite paintings are housed and stays inside the building until closing time. It is the very scene that she has imagined since she planned her Washington trip. There is some daylight left when she waves goodbye to the security guard. She catches an Uber back to the hotel and relaxes her exhausted feet.

The next morning, despite leaving the hotel later than the previous day, she enters the Renwick Gallery at 10 a.m., as soon as the gate opens. This contemporary gallery introduces her to a slew of talented contemporary artists. Surprisingly, she finds a Korean artist's ceramic work that looks woefully broken but awesome. Since her father asked Linda to purchase items related to the White House, she will drop by the White House Visitor Center to buy a couple of key chains and magnets.

Steven Young Lee, *Vase with Landscape and Dinosaurs*, 2014

She then takes the Metro and gets off at the Smithsonian Station. Because she is Asian, The Freer and Sackler Museums are must-see destinations. The majestic building makes her happy as she feels like the Asian art collection is treated honorably. She is surprised that many Caucasians are gazing upon very sophisticated crafts from China with a look of wonder.

According to Hoon's guidebook, the Castle was supposed to be the first stop. However, she thinks that it is also a good choice to visit the castle last. All her questions are answered here.

Lion with Rider 75 BCE - 50 CE

Katharina Fritsch *Hahn/Cock* 2010

Plan for 3-day Itinerary

Route: National Portrait Gallery, Hillwood Estate and Museum, National American History Museum
Visitors: Victor, a well-traveled 70-year-old male and his wife, who has knee-joint problems. They have come to D.C. to meet their son's fiancée.

During their stay in D.C., Victor wants to show his wife portraits of Barack and Michelle Obama. They are housed in the National Portrait Gallery near Chinatown. Although Victor can drive a car, they opt to use public transportation to avoid traffic. Because they begin their visit to this huge museum with a clear target, they waste no time getting to and enjoying the wonderful paintings.

On the second day, Hillwood Estate and Museum is the perfect destination for this old but enthusiastic couple. Victor went online and reserved discounted tickets for seniors. Luckily, there is a designated parking spot for the handicapped. He signs up for the mansion tour as well as a garden tour and he rents a wheelchair for his wife.

Victor recalled his wife talking about "The Wizard of Oz" and it just so happens that he had recently read an article about how the National Museum of American History has a dedicated gallery for Dorothy's Ruby Slippers. Before leaving the Hillwood Museum, Victor visits the American History Museum's website and finds the exact location of Dorothy's Ruby Slippers. Upon arrival, he asks a volunteer at the information desk where these popular shoes are. As a result, his wife is amazed by Victor's thoughtfulness and repays him with a wonderful smile.

Amy Sherald *First Lady Michelle Obama* 201

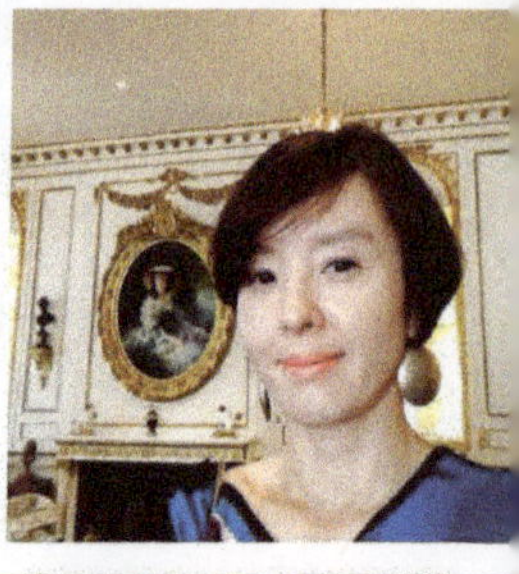

Plan for 4-day itinerary

Route: National Museum of Natural History, ARTECHOUSE, Holocaust Museum, Glenstone

Visitors: a 45-year-old single mom, Kim and her teenage daughter Rachel. Their relationship is fraught because Kim and her husband are in the middle of a divorce. Kim hopes to get back to the old happy days with her daughter.

Rachel usually gets up late in the morning like most teenagers. Lately, she has been rebelling against her mom. While Kim planned to visit one museum per day, there has been some serious bickering from the beginning of the trip. The reason Kim chose the Natural History Museum as today's destination is that her daughter Rachel loved reading "Night at the Museum" when she was a little girl. However, Rachel doesn't remember anything about it. She texts her friends instead of paying careful attention to the collection.

All the Smithsonian museums are rejected, but Rachel agrees to see one on the second day. ARTECHOUSE is very popular with young people who post photos of their visits on social media. Luckily Rachel's sulky look softens and they gain their smiles again.

The museum for the third day is the Holocaust Museum. As you know, this museum is not one for fun, Kim really wants Rachel to feel

the happiness about what they have now. Rachel says that the most impactful place is the hall dedicated to innocently dead people. She lights a candle for them and has a short silence. She silently thanks her family for keeping her safe and providing for her all these years.

The Glenstone is in the D.C. suburbs of Maryland. From the parking lot to the visitor center, Kim and Rachel don't talk. They are immersed in the scene that surrounds them. A newly built pavilion houses many pieces of contemporary art. When they get to the main gallery, there is a special exhibition of Louise Bourgeois who is famous for the "Maman Series." Bourgeois created large-scale sculpture and installation art, and she was also a prolific painter as well as a printmaker. Most of her artworks remind Rachel of pain and fear, and even after she leaves, it lingers in Rachel's mind. Mysteriously when she comes back home, Louise Bourgeois's art grows on Rachel. Maman is a bronze, stainless steel, and marble sculpture which depicts a spider. The title is a French

word for Mother. It alludes to the strength of Bourgeois's mother with imagery such as spinning, weaving, nurture, and protection. Rachel briefly transforms into someone who really loves to understand Kim, her mother.

Plan 5-day Itinerary

Route: Air and Space Museum (Udvar-Hazy center)
Visitors: Kaan, a 57- year- old male wants his family, including twins with mild mental problems, to enjoy their family trip safely

The family has had short trips before, but this is going to be their longest one yet. At first sight, his kids look normal. However, they often make a loud noise in public spaces, therefore his family does not typically go to crowded sites. Interestingly, his kids become calm and focused when it comes to aircrafts. The Steven F. Udvar-Hazy Center in Chantilly, Virginia is the companion facility to the Air and Space Museum on the National Mall. Since the location and features of this museum are better for Kaan's family, he reserved a hotel nearby.

On the first day, they visit the John L.Plueger Family Welcome Center to get important information and a guide for the museum. Thankfully, his kids seem very excited and happy. They have minimized baggage and are dressed comfortably to be ready for a lot of walking. He connects to the museum's Wi-Fi and learns more about the historic aircraft and space shuttles on display. Today's goal is to get familiar with the building, such as locating the restrooms, café, and gift shop.

The kids show more interest in what they like on the second day. One of the twins spends time studying World War II German Aviation, while the other prefers spaceships and satellites. In the museum, there is a food court where busy visitors will be able to take a break and satisfy their hunger with goodies. Kaan always brings water bottles for his kids. On the third day, two kids participate in a few hands-on programs which are very interactive as well as educational. Kaan finds out kite-flying is planned for the next day. On the final day, though the kids usually make uncontrollable sounds in the theatre, they do fairly well in the IMAX. They also visit the Donald D.Engen Observation Tower. Kaan's family has visited here successfully for 5 days. After they get home, Kaan smiles to see his kids painting about a trip full of fun and aircrafts.

Films set in museums

1. *Night at the Museum* 2006
2. *Night at the Museum: Battle of the Smithsonian* 2009
3. *Night At the Museum: Secret of the Tomb* 2014
4. *The Relic* 1997
5. *House of Wax* 1953
6. *How to Steal a Million* 1966
7. *Museum Hours* 2012
8. *The Thomas Crown Affair* 1999
9. *Topkapi* 1964
10. *One of Our Dinosaurs is Missing* 1975
11. *Bringing Up Baby* 1938
12. *The Da Vinci Code* 2013
13. *The Cookie Thief* 2015

Books featuring museums

1. *The Museum of Extraordinary Things* by Alice Hofman
2. *The Goldfinch* by Donna Tartt
3. *All the Light We Cannot See* by Anthony Doerr
4. *From the Mixed-up Files of Mrs. Basil E.Frankweiler* by E.L.Konigsburg
5. *The Night at the Museum* by Milan Trenc
6. *Fancy Nancy at the Museum* by Jane O'Connor
7. *Museum Trip* by Barbara Lehman
8. *Mr. Wilson's Cabinet of Wonder: Pronged Ants, Horned Humans, Mice on Toast, and Other Marvels of Jurassic Technology* by Lawrence Weschler
9. *Wonderstruck* by Brian Selznick
10. *Little Fires Everywhere* by Celeste Ng
11. *People of the Book* by Geraldine Brooks
12. *The Museum* by Susan Verde
13. *A Gentle Madness* by Nicholas A. Basbanes
14. *Museum ABC* by Metropolitan Museum of Art

Epilogue

Congratulations! You've now learned about 41 museums in D.C. You deserve my compliment and respect. I'd like to end by sharing my son's story with you. As far as I know, he is not a huge fan of museums. When he was a little boy, he used to visit only one museum with his grandfather. That was a special place which commemorated dead soldiers who fought during several wars in Korea. I questioned as to why they would stick to just one instead of visiting several museums in Seoul. Years later, I realized that his way was also good to enjoy museums. Each time he was in the museum, he explored a new subject. One week his interest was conventional weaponry in the Korean War, the next week he would be interested in different artifacts which could build up and expand his knowledge related to weapons in this area. Eventually he became a specialist on a specific theme. As my son and his grandfather became familiar faces, they were given the freedom to explore the museum more thoroughly. For example, they were often invited to VIP parties for special exhibits.

Who you go to a museum with is sometimes more critical than which museum you visit. Some museums with mediocre reputations are places of comfort for me just because of the people I go with. I am sure that my son's special museum reminds him of his grandpa's sweetness and love. Why don't you hang out in the museums with someone you like?

Large number of Washingtonians are ignorant of the value of the museums they have in their backyard. In this book, I've tried not to deliver only standard information to audiences, but to describe how I feel about these treasures. This book is not created by an omnipotent person who can control everything and guide you perfectly. It's rather a history of my challenge in D.C. for four years. I took all the pictures in this book myself. One photo that I would like to introduce last is of an old but very elegant couple whom I met in the Hirshhorn Museum. It is if they are saying "I will not quit my museum tour even though I have to sit on a wheelchair all the way!"

I am not lonely anymore. When I need the companionship of friends, I go to a museum. They always greet me like old companions. Now it is time to say good-bye. It's your turn to enjoy life in Washington D.C.

CPSIA information can be obtained
at www.ICGtesting.com
Printed in the USA
JSHW020250200220
4325JS00003B/7

9 781624 292446